COLORLESS CANVAS

ANTHOLOGY

LAFICTIONER

ISBN 979-888591053-8

This book has been published with all efforts taken to make the material error-free after the consent of the author. However, the author and the publisher do not assume and hereby disclaim any liability to any party for any loss, damage, or disruption caused by errors or omissions, whether such errors or omissions result from negligence, accident, or any other cause.

While every effort has been made to avoid any mistake or omission, this publication is being sold on the condition and understanding that neither the author nor the publishers or printers would be liable in any manner to any person by reason of any mistake or omission in this publication or for any action taken or omitted to be taken or advice rendered or accepted on the basis of this work. For any defect in printing or binding the publishers will be liable only to replace the defective copy by another copy of this work then available.

Neruda

Dedicated to everyone who wonders we are writing for them.

Yes, We are.

Contents

Contents

Do Check

www.lafictioner.com

Preface

"A piece of art is only justified if it's with one who understands the beauty of it."

Day 1, of me thinking to draft a book. A collection of art that would heal any soul.

I wish to write it all alone but my preoccupation with the marketing job did not allow me to draft anything as such. Why not an anthology? The very question and thought of it seemed a lot of work to me. I had several doubts regarding the working and prefacing of the book. But all that came to an end when I met a bunch of writing freaks. They were the ones who made Lafictioner what it is today.

We formed the basic idea of the anthology and started searching for poets. Soon we met Jahnavi, a young girl passionate about writing. She was running her own telegram page delicately pushing the content of the page every single day. She was the one who would send an email every single day reminding us and asking us about the progress of her draft. She gave her writings to us and helped us in every possible way that she could. Her writing was emotionally very difficult to generate at her age. She writes beyond the ability of mindset one has at her age.

Soon we found Tanya, I will call her story a mature tale. She initially was difficult to convince and took the time to submit the writeups. However, every masterpiece of art is a work of ages. Her writings are the ones that will make your thoughts fight back to your emotions. It's her words that carry a complete novel.

Lastly, it was my turn to finish the polish. It took me some time but I gave my best to carve the best of this diamond. Gave it a name colorless canvas. A place where you are the one to decide what to paint. A book where you decide what emotion to carve. A tale where you paint the story.

Thank You

Team Lafictioner.

The Authors

Tanya Soni

"Tanya Soni is a teen writer and learning enthusiast from Telangana.She is inquisitive, imaginative and believes in giving her time improving her skills.Her works are not restricted to a particular genre and never fails to impress the readers. Some of her admirable pomes are present in this publication "COLOURLESS CANVAS " hope you enjoy giving it a read. She loves to interact with her readers via her instagram @aze_al
"

Neruda

Lakshmi Jahnavi

"Lakshmi Jahnavi is a determined courageous teen writer. Writing is not just an escape but her passion. Started writing since 12, to date finished 250+ writeups on vivid topics. She believes that writing is an art of the heart. Her pen is just the means of communicating her emotions. Her writings are a waterfall of consciousness flowing with

pebbles of emotions and life experiences. ”

3

1. The Word of A Prisoner

I'm the one who is enjoying freedom in prison,
You are one who searches for independence in the open air.
I'm the one who speaks of beauty behind the bars,
You are one who quests for a smile being in the arms of charm,
I'm the one who paints the city red within four walls,
You are one who watch clock to celebrate in the jolly world,
I'm the one who is adoring the rainbow in pale white blot,
You are one who is in search of colors in a paint box,
I'm one who is spending happy hours in dark days of life,
And, you are one waiting to perish dark moments in happy hours of life,
I'm the one who is living with the assurance of death,
And you, my dear, are one who is dying assuming a better life.
The one thing creating contradiction is only in the way you and I think,
You have got all that you want,
But nothing which you could own,
And I've got all that I could own because I have never wished for any want.
Dear its life and the only thing important in life is life itself,
So, just smile.

- Tanya Soni

2. Dead Soul

I sat today again to write,
My words are expressing me,
My woes are sounding,
My eyes are dropping tiny morsels,
Here's my pen scribbling dark scripts on plane sheet,
And my thoughts expressing grief,
My heart is throbbing to attain peace,
My wounds are crossing limits: No heal.
I'm again alone in this vast world,
Some sit beside, speak and go.
Some go by,
Some have nil to say, and most don't care,
Me revolving around these malaises,
Meet situations only those: Fake.
My dreams admired; someone would stand along me,
Lift me back;
To lend a shoulder, so I could weep,
To cure my ailments, so I could grin,
But none came.
Just the rustling leaves and littered papers,
In dry season with dark rains,
Dull noon and cursed nights,

A fake smile and speechless cries.
I'm left with a living body and dead soul

- Tanya Soni

3. Dear Santa

I don't ask you to gift me big box of toys and chocolate bars,
I don't wish to get little dolls in my stocks,
I don't want comics, pencils, books, nor cars.
I don't demand for latest video games,
Nor for magic sticks nor for crayons.
My willing is not to gift me hairbands not even lip balms,
Nor lip-gloss, no foundation, or brush to get from you,
Not even a handbag not even an elegant boot,
Don't give me 6 inches heels,
No don't give me the Disney princess gown,
Nor do I need any glamours jewellery nor crown,
Nor I wish for any pleasant chimes,
I want no tea cups not any kind of draperies for my home,
Nor do I need any eye-catching frame,
Nor gift wall stickers to me,
Dear Santa;
Gift me no watch no clock no any object I need,
Gift me an option so I could thee,
I gift you some jellies, some cookies a piece of cake and a smile I gift thee,
As always shall you make happy

Take some cheers also from me, Gift me this chance to gift to thou,
Not in stockings but a grin on phiz.

- Tanya Soni

4. The Storeroom's Story

This is the way, how I explain the day when we met;
I was on huff & you kept apologizing me,
I had no speech & your words kept pleasing,
I had no interest & you kept showing yours,
When we fought & a misunderstanding disturbed our understanding;
I didn't except to come back again, to let that beauty to set, to feel that calmness again, to accept your care again,
I wanted to end.
What to do I had an ego problem.
But still you brought me back to our way,
To smile & leave all the stuff again,
How, we met in the store room?
Where Everything was calm, except your eyes.
Which expressed your feelings,
Everything was quiet, except your words which kept pleasing,
Everything laid swooned, except a heart which was longing to be fetched,
There was no cool breeze,
But still I felt something flowing to calm.
There was no sea,
But still I felt something ranging,

There was no light,
But I felt the brightness,
There was no feast,
But I felt to be in a fair,
There was nothing special to be described, nothing cute around.
But, your presence, made me feel so.
My fire was being slowly put off.
My anger had calmly dropped
My ego was simply killed,
I felt getting back to the one, I thought to reject.
This is a store room's story,
Where two hearts met.
One heart pumped while others functioned,
One's eyes wept and the other's smiled.
Both loved but,
One proposed and the other accepted.

- Tanya Soni

5. Not A Beggar

I rest below the elderly banyan tree
And busy roads,
I eat rotten foot, drink dirty water,
I wander every street,
To each house I go
I wear torn clothes,
Ruptured shoes are mine,
I own no shelter,
No house is mine,
No vacation I go to,
No business trip,
I held a bowl in my hand
And wish to get whatever you give,
I`m not as sound as you,
Nor I want to be as wealthy as you,
You don't offer me anything,
Please aid me to offer you something,
Take my understanding and possess this,
I'm not a beggar,
I'm just a unwealthy unhygienic man,
Sent by lord to keep a check at your humble and broad heart.

-Tanya Soni

6. Oyster

Don't ask me why I stay silent near the waves,
Don't question me why I gaze at the sea.
Don't ask how I remain still on the hot sand,
Don't question why I don't enjoy tides.
Don't ask why I don't smile with you guys,
Don't ask me anything.
I can't answer you,
My issues don't affect you.
I was an oyster deep inside the liquid.
The waves pushed me out and, now I'm afraid I can't go back.
And I'm afraid I will lose my sea, my fishes, my beach.
If you find me, I will be hung in your neck as an adornment piece.
I am quiet,
I am silent.

-Tanya Soni

7. Granny Tale

The cool breeze flew,
Flew my heart away with it,
We travelled till the sky,
Passing through the clouds leaving behind the sky,
I boarded a meteoroid
And it took me to the moon.
Moon over there dreaming of pace,
A smile on his face,
I broke his dream, the dream of the `Night King';
But, look how strange oh! So strange,
I was the queen he dreamed of,
Now, I'm there up in his kingdom.
The starts are lads and starts lassies,
Meteoroids are Courtiers and milky way is my palace,
This is the tale my grandma said, before she left to heaven.

-Tanya Soni

8. Still

You left me alone,
To this place, to this land.
For true; Nothing has changed,
OH! True Nothing'
The wind still teases my shirt it still passes through my hair,
The pieces of paper still run with it,
My tie still flows with it,
In the whoopy playground,
still people fall, still people run,
The sand of the ground still sunk into my shoes,
It's pebbles still trouble my sole,
The stairs are yet the same,
Boys and girls sit there still,
Gossips are still heard by the walls.
In noon the bell still rings,
Lunch boxes are shared today even,
Chasing for snacks are still seen,
The PT teacher still holds a stick,
Whistles and gestures are still followed,
The uniform gets dirty today even,
Pockets are torn today even,
Arguments are still there,

Cacophony still heard,
The blackboard, didn't shed its colour yet,
Dusters are yet borrowed,
Benches are yet carved, Erasers and pens are shared,
Papers and books are yet torn.
Absolutely Nothing has changed!
Yes! Nothing!
My ears still long to hear your voice in the winds,
My hair still gets disturbed, to listen your chuckles,
The tie still is untied, for you to set,
My shoes still let the sand rest on it, for your scolding's,
Lase still un-knot itself to hear your command,
Pebbles still struck in my socks, they still hurt.
The stairs still wait for you,
In gossips I still search your tone,
My heart still rings with the lunch bell,
The tap still rush water in them,
My face still waits for the water to splash.
And then my scenes wait for your laughter to evoke,
The uniform gets dusty even today,
I still wait for you to un-dust,
The chocolate still is in my hand for you to chase,
The whistle still makes me run,
In the noises I still search your voices,
I still wait for you near the gate.
Nothing has changed
First it was you, now your memories, you met an accident.

You left.

But I still wait for you.

-Tanya Soni

9. Who wetten's or Who dry's?

Who wetten's or Who dry's? was the name of the game,
The sea and the shore played.
Where I was the judge and was not a Dane,
The first turn of the sea which rage and rage, it's waves over the sun-burnt space.
And next the shore shed the water and gets back to its original face.
I stood at the edge of the water and ran on the sunk`y terrain as the sea splashes waves,
I kept saving me.
The game then took a twist now it wasn't the sea and the shore,
I wasn't the judge anymore,
As now it turned to `Me Vs Sea'
I competed with the waves'.
The game changed to "Who ran faster" me or the sea.
The water ran behind and I kept saving my feet,
Though it succeeded many a times.
I celebrated the winning with my whole life,
...Now was the shore was envy.
"I was the one who always played with this guy" it said,

And loosen its sand and try's to drop me in sea.
I felt worried and then left the place in a haste,
And again, the play being.
"Who wetten's or Who dry's"

Tanya Soni

10. And Then I Left

My heart bore some, unspoken pain,
Suffering were felt but not understood.
Nor thou, nor thy cared,
Couples and Covey were passers-by.
Some chuckling, some speaking spent the time,
My time awaited long but none came to understand my desolate,
Many I met, as days went by faces changed, and with each face emerged a new word.
But; No speech cured the cursed heart.
Later one night, besides the silent tides I sat,
The shore was clear as no one was there.
My weeps and loneliness paid me company,
I turned to the night king for him to insist.
But, for dull fate he was on leave.
It was a complete dark night,
As thunder clouds sealed the sky.
No soothing breeze was felt, nor at a sight anyone met.
I was all alone on the dead sunken stage,
Then after a while a thought knocked the shutters of my mind,
Which later instructed me to just hold on myself and start healing alone.

-Tanya Soni

11. The Decayed Is Brood

I have traveled miles, on the road of life.
The dust of wisdom,
The print of foolishness I've seen.
Dried ocean and
Flooded desert I've seen.
Police station owned by a thief,
Judges behind bars I've seen.
Freeze of sun and,
Winter heat has seen.
In autumns the canopy,
In monsoon dried trees I've seen.
Diamonds in bin and,
Jewells of glass I've seen.
Dim stars and,
Moon self-lit I've seen.
I've seen the glaciers thirsty,
The potable seas I've seen.
Kings in quest of alms and,
Beggars on chariots I've seen.
Garden on a brick and,
Empty nourished lands I've seen.
Carved soil and, Painted ice I've seen,

what I've seen, you must have seen too.
What I speak is true,
Ere-day yesterday do know.
Nothing today is new,
The decayed is still brood.
The flourished is yet crude.

-Tanya Soni

12. T-T-ToTo

As long as I thought of pets there were so many,
But I never thought of a little pretty tortoise which bore at top belly.
It hid its head inside its belly,
And then suddenly come out without me calling Pearly.
It pushes the water back and back,
Feeling as it's on a marathon track.
It's bulging eyes feels to me some scary,
Yet, many times it makes me feel merry.
Naming it was not easy, I wanted it to be fancy.
My buddies all quest for my tortoise name, No doubt it gained a lot of fame.
One said O-O-OLO, one said R-R-RUBO.
Someone said S-S-SUMO, and the other named E-E-ELOO
But, in the end it was named by me T-T-TOTO.

-Tanya Soni

13. Old Age

I agree with you, mirror.
You tell me truth, I look fine.
Show me what's true, you are loyal.
Someday I dressed gorgeous, you made me grin,
Someday I was untied, you reflected my bad,
I must not blame you,
You show what you see.
Be great what it means.
Day after day you show me my scars.
Yeah! It's true I'm ageing.
My mush doesn't flash those young age charms now.
My eyes must not show you that glitters.
All fine! I agree
I don't look that beautiful now.
But dear; MIRROR.
I fear sometimes, can I have faith in you?
Yes', you must be surprised I didn't ever speak'th so, yet dear agree now.
This is me, over the years my skin wrinkled, my hairs grew grey and for the fact of age; I'm old now.
Over the years my I'm changed,

I don't disagree I look fishy now. But dear reflector My soul never drifted,
my heart still bore the same feeling.
The same care, The same love.
Why then this bad to me?
Till yesterday the one son I loved,
I lived for, left me here in old age?
Why don't you show him my soul?
Why can't you reflect my throbs?
Or
Am I that ugly he couldn't, see?
Is my heart filled with dust?

-Tanya Soni

14. Trust Me It Still Exists

The moon was hidden,
Thunders sounds,
Tapering rain,
Through that street water rushes,
There was none.
That was a violent night,
There was only I,
Tensed and shivering,
To save me I tried.
There and here all shops shutters shut.
Total alone streets, no wheelers, no horn.
Time was turning rains to storms,
Troubled I was
Throat was dry,
Then in while,
Two eyes protrude to me,
Throbbing my soul out of fear,
There it was a car,
Twain boots came to me,
Towel was warped to me,
Took me into wheeler
Tea he asked served me in bowel

We travelled to his house
To his room I was taken
Two cookies two Pisces, I was served.
This human saved me
Tale of mine is true,
Thereof I believe humanity Trust me it still exists.
Therein who saves an abandoned dog.

-Tanya Soni

15. Will The Inspector?

Will the black mustache inspector, who holds a stick, help me out?
Will he bang the trees?
Will he arrest the breeze?
Will he warn the stupid shining stone?
ill-treat the dawn chirping bird?
No, guesses for what he is gonna do,
But I have filed a complaint, against the one treating me like a BRAT!!!!

-Tanya Soni

16. The Life

Life isn't easy for everyone. How wonderful is that when we think about this whole world?
While walking on the roads we see many are coming and going.
We walked along to see magics.
Many reasons, many causes, many prayers, many excuses, many feelings, many droughts, many waves of anger,
Many problems, many revolts, many sacrifices, many compliments, many compromises, many greetings, many celebrations, many more made us.
How lucky we are??
Many things made us but don't let one thing ruin us.

-Lakshmi Jahnavi

17. Affinity

Your eyes represent my vision,
Your heart became my habitat,
Your soul became my kingdom,
Your possessiveness became my solider,
Your lap became my cushion,
Your love became my world,
Your smile became my touch,
Your promises became my blessings,
Your sorrow becomes my curse,
You are my boon,
And
I hope I will withstand that boon.

-Lakshmi Jahnavi

18. Inner Feelings

Sometimes I wanna be dumb because I can't answer all your questions.
At least just once try to understand my innerness it has a lot to see and say.
It is dying always.
After all, I understood it is not dying. Many being killed.
It needs freedom, care, love.
It needs many but it can't express because it turned into a stone.
Whenever it needs happiness, it get tears as a gift.
At least once it needs smile as a reward.

-Lakshmi Jahnavi

19. Lets Experience

I am surprised by the offers that we get from society.
We are living with the fear of failure.
If once we fail,
We aren't losers,
We are just beginners.
Oh my God,
Society tags us very badly and scares us very much
People who are dealing with that fear can experience neither success nor failure.
They are living as a dead ones.
Experience every part of life.
Don't fear failing.
Don't fear to win.
Don't fear to face.

-Lakshmi Jahnavi

20. Pen Your Life

Life is not a game to win or lose.
It's a book to write new chapters always.
I repeat.
Life is an empty book to write new different chapters.
A book with different pens and inks.
Decorate the book with colors called feelings.
-Lakshmi Jahnavi

21. Hard Emotions

Hours of conversation are useless when the mouth speaks but the heart lies mute.
Spending hours with others is useless when the soul lies with the other.
Sometimes precious eyes speak louder than words.
But only some pretty and mesmerizing eyes and souls can understand those words.
The remaining ones can't even imagine.

-Lakshmi Jahnavi

22. Accept The Fear

The fear to start something is very awful.
That fear keeps us unstable.
We can't start anything with that fear.
Again we feel pity for us that we had not yet started.
This fear is hideous.
Every moment of our life is challenging.
Let's accept this fear.

-Lakshmi Jahnavi

23. The Sense of Being

Being wrong in situations.
Being right in situations.
It depends on the vision that others see.
You are right
or
You are wrong.
It's right or wrong life had put you there, it's your responsibility to withstand.
Everything has two faces good and bad.
But vision plays a major role.
It's all about vision towards positivity.

-Lakshmi Jahnavi

24. Miss You

The way you see,
The way you smile,
The way you write,
The way you read,
The way you scold,
The way you eat,
The way you fight,
The way you speak,
The way you went to the peak.
The way you were, will be always memorable.
You may go away from us, your body may be cremated, but your soul will always be with us.
"God took you from this world but he can't take you from our hearts and souls.

-Lakshmi Jahnavi

25. Pain

The pain,
That breaks you,
That harms you,
That beats you,
That pokes you,
That teaches you,
That literate you,
That promotes you,
That even kills you,
It is all that you do after pain.

-Lakshmi Jahnavi

-

26. Unsaid Feelings

I see you,
I get tears, those represent you.
You are eternal.
That tear signifies you.
I can't tell you,
I can't hide from you.
My mouth can't speak.
But my eyes do.
When you see them you understand the purity of my love.

-Lakshmi Jahnavi

27. Unspoken

I really want to die.
Not for the fear of facing society,
But for the fear of facing myself.
I really want to die.
Not for the fears of incompleteness,
But for the fear of regrets.
I really want to die.
Not for the fear of relations,
But for the converses.
I really want to die.
Not for the helplessness,
But for the self-tackleness.

-Lakshmi Jahnavi

28. The Devotion

The eternal spiritual power.
Controls us,
Relaxes us,
Praises us,
We call it devotion.
And that devotion towards the power gives many hopes to us.
And that devotion gives the exact meaning of completeness of life
is attained and explained through that devotion.

-Lakshmi Jahnavi

29. Hoping For an Eternal Destiny

Not trying to stop me.
Not trying to start for me.
Not trying to get defeated.
Not trying to get succeeded.
Not trying to accept the situations.
Not trying to overcome the situations.
Not trying to welcome.
Not trying to shun.
Just trying to watch and digest the things.
Hoping for an eternal destiny.

-Lakshmi Jahnavi

30. From an Idea to Ideal

From holding father's hand and walking,
To holding difficulties and crawling.
From the dare that, my father lifts me,
To the fear that I am nothing if I fall.
From learning lessons from father,
To leaning on with responsibilities.
Life changes from being an innocent kid to a human with responsibilities and accountability.
From an idea to ideal.

-Lakshmi Jahnavi

31. Way of Sight

Seen a pigeon from the window of my room.
Got shocked at how beautiful it is.
Its neck is so realistic and how many colors it is showing through its neck.
Oh, my pigeon,
How pretty are you?
Sometimes some awkward things happen.
Regularly seen things sometimes it become the most beautiful scenes in life.
Change the way of sight.
Sometimes everything becomes beautiful.

-Lakshmi Jahnavi

32. Where We Are Going?

Trying to escape from nature is what we are doing now.
What is life?
Many say Problems.
Many say solutions.
Many say pain.
Many say happiness.
Many say feelings.
But I feel life is a gift.
A gift from nature to explore it.
But we are seeking privacy from nature.
Imagine once what if nature takes privacy.
Stay close to nature.
Don't destroy nature.
Explore Nature.

-Lakshmi Jahnavi

33. My Brothers

My first enemy.
My first love.
My first gift.
My first savior.
My first quarreling partner.
My first best friend.
My first problem solver.
My problem creator.
My trainer.
My painer.
Oh, my brother.
My life trainer.
My life reliever.

-Lakshmi Jahnavi

34. The Words

The world is fascinating with the words.
Words can break you and make you.
Words can steal your heart,
Words can break your heart.
The right use in a certain place can even appreciate us.
Words and timing are the correct definitions to get appreciation or to get insulted.
The words,
Makes us,
Breaks us,
Heals us,
Answers us,
Questions us,
Relieves us,
Praises us,
Raises us,
Motivate us.
Anything can be done through words.
I repeat, anything.
But we should know the appropriate use and we should use words in a disciplined manner.
Your words may describe yourself.

Be aware of words.

-Lakshmi Jahnavi

35. Self-Consideration

Congratulations to myself.
Kudos to myself.
Greetings to myself.
Wishes to myself.
Thanks to myself.
Self-esteem.
Self-conscious.
Self-conquering.
Self-confidence.
Self-control.
Self-positioning.
Self-liberating.
Self-space.
Yes, self-things are sometimes important.
When we turn back at a particular time, we should not feel pity for ourselves.
We should feel proud for all those things that we have done for ourselves because if you fail to satisfy yourself, how can you satisfy a so-called person?

-Lakshmi Jahnavi

36. As Long As We Are

As long as we are alive there is no death.
As long as we are happy there is no sadness.
As long as we are sad there is no happiness.
As long as we are crying there is no smiling.
As long as we are comfortable there is no uncomfortable.
As long as we are talking there are no dumb.
As long as what we are doing there is no opposite thing.
So as long as we do negative things, we won't be able to see positive things.
Let's do positive things with positive minds.

-Lakshmi Jahnavi

37. Pure Friendship

That freedom to scold.
That freedom to tease.
That freedom to care.
That freedom to hang on.
That freedom to hug.
That freedom to hurt.
That freedom to cure.
That freedom comes from the deep feeling called friendship.
Let's explore friendship that has no boundaries.
Friendship is the magic of foreverness.

-Lakshmi Jahnavi

38. Wanna Be A Star

I wanna be a star.
Not to be so close to the moon, but also to be high in the sky.
I wanna be a star.
Not to see how other stars are glowing.
But also, to see my shine and brightness.
I wanna be a star.
Not to be an icon,
But to be a role model.
I wanna be a star.
Not to think that I will not shine in the mornings.
But to wonder that I am amazing, twinkling at night.
I wanna be a star.
Not to see people from the top but to feel the heights that man can reach,
I wanna be a star.
Not to look beautiful near the sea but to wonder the beauty that nature has.
I wanna be a star.
Not to navigate,
But to show one's path.

-Lakshmi Jahnavi

39. Brittle Walls

They are lost.
Those noises don't hear me anymore,
The football doesn't hit me nowadays,
Nobody scratches or carves on me,
No splashes of water paints nor crayons,
Papers are not glued on me.
Corners are no more cleared,
I'm not coloured anymore,
No one hit me with nails,
No body script their names on me anymore.
There is no one sheltered here during freezing days,
No body rest here in thunder storms,
The plug holes in me are dead.
The book self, the cellar, the utensils are not disturbed anymore.
Creases of door don't make noise,
Nor windows are closed to save from cold,
Just climes dingle with minute strokes of wind,
Mice strode in and patagium flatter nights and days.
There even lies a nest in the grooves of mine,
The bird and hatchlings stay in it.
Some days I listen theirs chirps and muse over the unflushed past,

Those little kids their mother and his husband, they stayed in here.
Oh! How well they lived.
What was wrong from my side?
Those chatters, why are they silent now?
Well, they say walls bear ears.
What shall these ears hear now?
The gossips, the chatters, the laughs are all muted.
Whom should these walls of this barren house,
Explain the ubiquitous solely of each corner of the chamber?
They were ephemeral. But, soaked in their memories in each brick of this concrete wall.
They are gone, without breaking even a brick,
Still, they made the walls brittle by leaving behind their reflections.

-Tanya Soni

40. Thank you, God

Hey God,
You made us,
You named us,
You pained us,
You taught us,
You trained us,
You happied us,
You cared us,
You slapped us,
You clapped at us,
You divided us,
You united us,
You empowered us,
You praised us,
At last,
You called us to come to
We are eagerly waiting for your call.
Because we can't live without you.
And our Destination is you.
Amen.

-Lakshmi Jahnavi

www.lafictioner.com

Printed by Libri Plureos GmbH in Hamburg, Germany